HOMELESS

Youth Living on the Streets

Gail Snyder

ReferencePoint
Press

San Diego, CA

About the Author

Gail Snyder is a freelance writer and advertising copywriter who has
written more than twenty-five books for young readers. She has a
degree in journalism from Pennsylvania State University and lives in
Chalfont, Pennsylvania, with her husband, Hal Marcovitz.

For more information, contact:
ReferencePoint Press, Inc.
PO Box 27779
San Diego, CA 92198
www.ReferencePointPress.com

LIBRARY OF CONGRESS CATALOGING-IN-PUBLICATION DATA

Names: Sydner, Gail, author.
Title: Homeless : youth living on the streets / Gail Sydner.
Description: San Diego : ReferencePoint Press, 2021. | Includes
    bibliographical references and index. | Audience: Ages 14-18
Identifiers: LCCN 2021016102 (print) | LCCN 2021016103 (ebook) | ISBN
    9781678201708 (library binding) | ISBN 9781678201715 (ebook)
Subjects: LCSH: Homeless youth--Juvenile literature. | Street
    youth--Juvenile literature. | Homeless youth--Social
    conditions--Juvenile literature.
Classification: LCC HV4493 .S93 2021 (print) | LCC HV4493 (ebook) | DDC
    362.7/75692--dc23
LC record available at https://lccn.loc.gov/2021016102
LC ebook record available at https://lccn.loc.gov/2021016103

CONTENTS

Hiding in Plain Sight

Although only seventeen years old, Cori Dixon of Philadelphia has felt as though she carries the weight of the world on her shoulders. She has already lived in a homeless shelter with her mother, moved in with another family member with whom she did not get along, slept on a shower curtain on the floor of a dilapidated apartment, lived on the street by herself, and signed herself into an emergency shelter.

Dixon wishes that she could be a "normal" teenager for whom home is a place where there is food in the refrigerator, snacks in the pantry, at least one parent or grandparent to provide supervision, a bedroom with a comfortable bed, and a closet for her clothes. "I feel like a 50-year-old woman, I've been through so much," says Dixon. "I just wanted to be a teenager for a while."[1]

Dixon is one of thousands of homeless youths whose chaotic lives lead them to move frequently with or without their parents to homeless shelters, motels, or homes of relatives and friends or to seek refuge in abandoned houses or on the streets. Housing insecurity among young people is a global problem that affects teens who live in cities and rural areas. Says Ellen Bassuk, a psychiatrist at Harvard Medical School in Cambridge, Massachusetts, and founder of the National Center on Family Homelessness, "Homelessness is a traumatic experience for people because they lose everything. They lose their routines, privacy, friends, and pets. They are in situations where they don't know where the next meal is going to come from, or where they're going to be tomorrow."[2]

Confusing Statistics

For many reasons, it is not easy to pinpoint exactly how many young people in America are considered homeless. One reason is that there are differing definitions of what it means to be homeless. For example, statistics compiled by the US Department of Housing and Urban Development (HUD), the government agency that funds programs to address homelessness, count a young person as homeless if he or she is not a full-time resident of a house or apartment. Under that definition, there were more than 107,000 homeless young people in 2018, the last year for which statistics are available.

HUD does not count as homeless the young people and their families who double up with relatives or friends, sharing their living spaces—a common occurrence that reflects housing instability. This discrepancy is significant, according to Barbara Duffield, executive director of SchoolHouse Connection, a Washington, DC–based organization that helps find places to live for homeless young people. She says, "The HUD numbers are seen as official numbers. They are what mayors pay attention to. I think they are what private philanthropy pays attention to. I think the HUD numbers drive policy. I think that's tragic."[3]

> "I feel like a 50-year-old woman, I've been through so much. I just wanted to be a teenager for a while."[1]
>
> —Cori Dixon, seventeen-year-old homeless teen

But some groups offer even narrower definitions of homelessness for young people. The National Center for Homeless Education, an agency of the US Department of Education that helps schools provide education for homeless young people, placed the number of homeless public school students at 1.3 million during the 2018–2019 school year. That number only includes twelve- to twenty-four-year-olds not living with their parents.

Another organization that has stud-
ied homelessness among young people is
Chapin Hall, a research center at the University of Chicago. From 2015 through 2017,
Chapin Hall looked at the problem of homelessness among young people in America
and concluded that one in thirty people age
thirteen to seventeen experience homelessness each year, with
at least 25 percent of those young people doubling up with relatives or friends. For young people age seventeen to twenty-five,
the numbers rose to one in ten, with half of those older youths
living with friends. The lack of uniform statistics affects government policy, funding, and outreach efforts. Says US representative
Steve Stivers of Ohio, "If you don't count somebody as homeless,
you can't get them help."[4]

Hunger, Abuse, and Mental Illness

Whether counted or uncounted, homeless youths face a variety
of unpleasant circumstances that impact their present and future

*Thousands of homeless youths
move frequently to homeless
shelters or homes of relatives
and friends, or seek refuge on the
streets. Housing insecurity among
young people is a global problem.*

lives. Because they often look no different than youths and teens who have permanent homes, they may seem invisible even as they cope with problems beyond their years. Those problems include hunger, physical abuse, mental health issues, difficulty with school, and drug abuse.

Among the homeless teens who have faced such problems is Cori Dixon, who has not had a permanent home since she was five years old. Dixon says she has often suffered from anxiety and depression and at times has considered suicide. For years she had little interest in going to school. "What was the point of school?" she asks. "I had no focus, no peace."[5]

Life has improved somewhat for Dixon. As she entered her senior year at a Philadelphia high school, she aimed to improve her grades and eventually enroll in college. But as her senior year commenced, she still found herself living in a homeless shelter—a way of life she has yet to find a way to escape.

CHAPTER 1

Why Do Some Young People Lack Homes?

Natalie grew up in a rural region of Washington State, yet "big-city" problems found her after the fourteen-year-old's father left his family. Upset by her husband's abandonment, Natalie's mother found comfort in drugs and alcohol, leaving Natalie in charge of her four younger brothers and sisters. "If she wasn't drunk or high, she was gone,"[6] Natalie says. As any young teenager would, the girl struggled with the responsibility of meeting her needs and those of her family members. The middle school student soon fell behind on her schoolwork.

She dropped out of school and became friendly with people who used methamphetamine, a popular drug that is highly addictive and known to cause users to lose their ambition. By the time she was seventeen, Natalie was no longer welcome at home, particularly by her mother's new boyfriend. Natalie was homeless. She was willing to go wherever she could find a place to stay, sometimes exchanging sex for a place to sleep. Sometimes she slept in an outdoor shed. Her situation was so dire that when she ended up in juvenile detention after being arrested, a development that most teens would dread, she found herself welcoming the experience because she knew she would have a bed and food to eat. Still, she dreamed about the normal life she had known before her father left and her mother fell into addiction. She says, "I want to be home with my mom, and I want to stop using, and I want to be clean with my mom. I want to be able to see my siblings."[7]

The circumstances that led to Natalie's homelessness and its horrors are not unique. They are shared by many other young people who find themselves enduring a chaotic home life, parental abandonment, mental health issues, addiction, and reliance on criminal activities to earn money.

> "I want to be home with my mom, and I want to stop using, and I want to be clean with my mom. I want to be able to see my siblings."[7]
>
> —Natalie, homeless teen

Homelessness Among the LGBTQ Community

One common characteristic among many young people who live on the streets is that they feel like outcasts from society. Often this feeling arises even before they become homeless. This is true of many LGBTQ youth, who leave their home because they find themselves no longer accepted by their parents and other family members.

Young people in the LGBTQ community make up a small fraction of the teen population—just 7 percent—but they account for up to 40 percent of homeless youth. When young people come out to their parents—meaning they disclose their sexual orientation or gender identity—as many as half of them find their news is met with disapproval, according to the New York City–based advocacy group True Colors United. Says Nick Seip, a True Colors United staff member, "Conflict within the family is one of the most frequently cited reasons young people experience homelessness. For lesbian, gay, bisexual, and transgender youth, the conflict is often around their sexual orientation or gender identity."[8]

Among the young people in the LGBTQ community who left home was Elegance Bratton. When he was sixteen years old, his parents learned he was gay. They soon pressured him to start dating girls. Unwilling to live his life according to their expectations, Bratton chose to leave his family's home in Jersey City, New Jersey. Bratton fled to nearby New York City, where he

Young people in the LGBTQ community account for up to 40 percent of homeless youth. This is because they leave their homes when they find themselves no longer accepted by their parents.

discovered a community of other people like him—people who were Black and gay—in the city's Christopher Street area.

Bratton spent the next ten years of his life wandering New York City streets—homeless yet at least feeling part of a community of other young people who shared his lifestyle. "I landed in a place where, for the first time in my life, people were excited to see all of me," he says. "The fact that I was gay was celebrated; the fact that I was a Black male was celebrated. It was the first time in my life where my intersectional identities were really able to co-mingle, and I felt like a complete person."[9] Bratton was eventually able to find a career and a home. He enrolled in college, and after graduation he pursued a career as a filmmaker.

As a young Black man, Bratton was a member of another demographic pushing him toward homelessness. Black youth

"The fact that I was gay was celebrated; the fact that I was a Black male was celebrated."[9]

—Elegance Bratton, former homeless teen

have an 83 percent greater chance of being homeless than young people who are White. Poverty is one reason for widespread homelessness among the community of young Black people, but financial hardship is not the sole reason for homelessness among Black youth. Additional problems that factor into the higher rate of homelessness for Black teens are issues such as housing discrimination, higher rates of incarceration among Black family members, a higher school dropout rate, and a greater likelihood that a Black youth will have spent time in the criminal justice system or foster care. Says a report by the MacArthur Foundation, a Chicago, Illinois–based organization that studies social issues, "More than one-third of homeless youth report prior involvement with the juvenile justice system and more than half reported being arrested since turning 18. . . . Youth of color make up one-third of adolescents in the US but two-thirds of juveniles who are incarcerated."[10]

The Failures of Foster Care

Among the factors that lead young Black people, as well as many other youths, into homelessness are the failures of the foster care system in America. According to the US Department of Health and Human Services, about 437,000 young people were living in foster care in 2018. And according to a study by the Baltimore, Maryland–based Annie E. Casey Foundation, in 2018 Black youths made up 14 percent of the childhood population in America, yet they accounted for 23 percent of the young people in foster care.

The foster care system is intended to provide a safety net for young people whose parents can no longer care for them. These reasons may include the death of parents or other caregivers, such as grandparents—circumstances that occur in the lives of one-third of youths in foster care. Other reasons that lead to young people being sent to foster homes include physical abuse by their parents, drug or alcohol addictions by their parents, abandonment by their parents, and the incarceration of their parents.

When these factors occur, local social services agencies run by city or county governments step in—often at the direction of the courts—to take custody of the young people and find homes for them with foster parents.

Foster parents awarded care of young people are provided with financial assistance from those government agencies to meet the needs of the youths in their care. Social workers are assigned to each case. They find foster parents willing to care for young people—sometimes in private homes but other times in group homes, which provide housing for several foster youths.

Foster care parents are legal guardians until the young person's parents can resume responsibility for his or her care or the young person in their care reaches age eighteen. The arrangement is not meant to last, and its temporary status makes it more difficult for young people to experience stable home lives. And while many young people do develop healthy and loving relationships with their foster parents, many young people never find themselves comfortable in their foster homes. Certainly, some foster parents fail to do an adequate job of meeting the needs of the young people in their care. And some foster care placements end up being as traumatic as the original situations that led to the child or adolescent being removed from the care of their parents. A young woman named Amy says she spent seven years in several foster homes and seldom found foster parents to be loving individuals. Instead, in her experience, her foster parents were often stern and demanding. She says, "A foster child is already taught that you don't speak up. It's dangerous. And don't forget that mom or dad already gave you up, so best to shut your mouth, or you could end up moving again."[11]

> "A foster child is already taught that you don't speak up. It's dangerous."[11]
>
> —Amy, former foster child

Aging Out of Foster Care

Even in the best cases, though, in which young people in foster care do find loving and caring environments, when they reach age

Coming Out Cost Him His Home

Each year about 550,000 youths and young adults under age twenty-five spend at least a week in homelessness, according to the Washington, DC–based nonprofit, the National Alliance to End Homelessness. Chasten Buttigieg, a gay youth, was one of them. In high school he tried to keep a low profile. Still, his fellow students made homophobic comments. After starting community college, Chasten summoned the courage to tell his parents he was gay. Rather than speak to them, he told them in a letter.

Chasten, who is now married to US secretary of transportation Pete Buttigieg, recalls that his mother wept at the news, his father was silent, and his brothers made loud objections. The resultant tense atmosphere led Chasten to abruptly leave home. For a few months, he cobbled together a hasty arrangement of couch surfing and living in his car, until his mother begged him to come home. His parents were able to accept his homosexuality, but the rift with his brothers has endured. His younger brother Dustin says, "We never got over it. I want the best for him. I just don't support the gay lifestyle."

Experts note that being gay is not a lifestyle. It is as much a part of who a person is as one's height, weight, and hair color.

Quoted in Ellen McCarthy, "Chasten Buttigieg Has Been a Homeless Community College Student and a Starbucks Barista. Now, He Could Be 'First Gentleman,'" *Washington Post*, May 1, 2019. www.washingtonpost.com.

eighteen they no longer qualify for foster care. Once they reach that age, the social service agencies cease providing financial aid to their foster parents. In most cases this means they must leave the system and go out on their own, even though they may be unprepared to live independently. Some twenty-three thousand young people a year find themselves aging out of the foster care system, and many of them become homeless. That is how Kevinee Gilmore found herself scared, homeless, and without skills at age eighteen. Her foster mother could no longer keep her once her living expenses were no longer covered.

Gilmore had been placed in foster care when her mentally ill mother and abusive stepfather were deemed unfit parents and

Homeless Shelters Are for Families Too

Not all homeless young people end up on the streets. Many actually live in homeless shelters with their families. Families sometimes turn to homeless shelters when parents separate or divorce, or when they lose their job, or when they cannot pay the rent or mortgage.

Family shelters have many rules. One common rule is that children can only live in a family shelter with their parents up to the age of twelve or thirteen. Older children may need to stay with relatives or in a shelter devoted to their age group.

This has been changing thanks to the Homeless Emergency Assistance and Rapid Transition to Housing Act (HEARTH). Passed by Congress in 2009, the act requires federally funded shelters to accept entire families regardless of the age of the children. Steve Berg, vice president of programs and policy for the National Alliance to End Homelessness says: "In the long run, the family is going to be a greater resource for these children than the homeless shelter. So if you have a choice between policies that make it easier to run the homeless shelter and the policies that make the family more intact, it's vastly more important to keep the family as a functioning entity that supports the kid."

Quoted in Caitlin Yoshiko Kandil, "For Many Homeless Families, a Tough Choice: Separation, or a Shelter Bed?" California Health Report, May 9, 2018. www.calhealthreport.org.

her grandmother was too sick to care for her. The foster care system left her traumatized.

The experience of waiting to be placed in foster care for the first time never left her. She says, "I vividly remember waiting with the social worker for someone to take me to my new home. It was the first of 13 placements. I attended five different high schools and only passed the 9th-grade proficiency test in the 12th grade. I hardly had any friends. Each time I got a little comfortable in a foster home, I got kicked out. I hated my life. I never got a chance to be a kid."[12]

Ill equipped to be on her own, Gilmore sometimes sought out the services of shelters and learned that some gave preference to young women who were pregnant. Desperate to get off the street, Gilmore often told administrators at the shelters that she was pregnant so she would have food and a place to sleep for a few nights.

Teen Pregnancy

According to statistics kept by Chapin Hall, 44 percent of homeless women who are age eighteen to twenty-five are pregnant or the mothers of young children. Moreover, 18 percent of homeless males in the same age group are parents. Pregnancy and parenthood are very challenging circumstances even for young people who have stable homes. In many cases, though, parents of pregnant teens may be unwilling to help them, leading to their pregnant daughters leaving home for life on the streets.

Ryan J. Dowd runs a homeless shelter in Chicago known as Hesed. One morning he arrived at the shelter at 7:30 a.m. to find a young teenager crying in the parking lot. She told Dowd that her

Many homeless women who are between the ages of eighteen and twenty-five are pregnant or the mothers of young children. Parents of pregnant teens may be unwilling to help them, often forcing them onto the streets.

father had driven her to the shelter that cold morning and left her alone and freezing because she was pregnant. With her were two large garbage bags containing all her possessions. Dowd recalls:

> I picked up the garbage bags and they immediately tore, spilling their contents all over the ground. Staring at this girl's stuff, I suddenly felt the full gravity of the moment, a moment that would likely define her life (for good or ill). Here was her childhood, scattered about on a homeless shelter's parking lot: six teddy bears, a chemistry book, a lime-green tennis racket, a few bras that wouldn't fit her in a few months, sunglasses with leopard print frames, and a pink diary with the heart clasp dangling precariously from when it had been pried off with a knife or screwdriver.[13]

Teenagers and young adults who face homelessness often do so for multiple reasons. Whether forced to leave home because of fears for their safety, told to leave by parents who are indifferent or unable to provide for them, or chafing at the rules set by parents and guardians who do not understand them, these young people can be found in virtually every community in America.

CHAPTER 2

What Is It like to Be a Homeless Teen?

By age fourteen, Eddie Martinez had already spent years living in room 219 at the Country Inn, a motel in San Bernardino, California. As a young child, Martinez had lived with his parents in a comfortable rented home in Oregon. But that lifestyle ended when his father shot a man and was sentenced to a prison term. Martinez's mother moved in with a boyfriend; they soon relocated to San Bernardino, but life did not get any easier. Martinez's mother was eventually arrested and imprisoned, leaving Martinez alone with the boyfriend, who is a drug abuser, at the Country Inn.

Martinez is not the only homeless teen who lives at the Country Inn. Many other young people live there as well with the remnants of their families. The families pay $280 a week for the rooms, usually out of the checks they receive from California's public assistance program. (Commonly known as welfare, under public assistance programs states typically provide cash payments to adults who are unable to find employment.)

Sam Maharaj, the manager of the motel, does what he can for many of the homeless teens and children who live there. He often buys pizzas for them when he suspects they have not been eating, provides maid service to keep their rooms clean, and summons the police if he suspects tenants are dangerous people. Still, the motel is located in a run-down neighborhood. Drug dealers stand on nearby corners. Prostitutes ply their trade in the rooms at the Country Inn. In the parking lot, Martinez and his friends play games and ride their bikes.

To express his feelings, Martinez often writes notes to himself then stuffs those notes into his backpack. On one note he wrote, "The only thing I haven't lost yet is my life. But I hope I'll lose it soon 'cause I can't take it anymore."[14]

Martinez's father was eventually released from jail. He found a job as a construction worker and was able to restart his life and find a permanent home. He traveled to San Bernardino, retrieved his son, and brought him home to Oregon. Soon after arriving in Oregon, Martinez wrote on his Facebook page, "School was fun today."[15]

Loss of Identity

Martinez and the other young people who have lived in places like the Country Inn are not unique. According to the Arlington, Virginia–based advocacy group National Center on Family Homelessness, nearly one hundred thousand teens and younger children in America live in cheap motel rooms. While living at the Country Inn, Martinez often experienced hunger, depression, and bullying. His schoolwork suffered. As the note in his backpack illustrates, he often hoped his life would end.

But even though his father rescued him and returned him to a stable home in Oregon, Martinez may continue to feel the effects of the trauma of his former life of homelessness. According to University of Toronto public health researcher Katherine Boydell, the experience of homelessness can interfere with a young person's self-image. Since adolescence is a time when identity is formed, she says, this interference is especially impactful. Says Boydell, "Homelessness means a loss of social identity—loss of permanent address, work, school, relationships, and place to call one's own. On a personal level, homelessness can mean a loss of self. Homelessness involves much more than not having a place to live. Individuals often lose their sense of identity, self-worth, and self-efficacy."[16]

Life on the Streets

Although Martinez faced challenges while living in a motel room, at least he knew that at the end of the day there would be a roof over his head and a bed in which to spend the night. Many young people who are homeless lack those guarantees. They literally live on the streets—meaning they never know where they will spend the night. It may be on the couch in a friend's home or in a homeless shelter or even on a bench in a public park. Moreover, they do not know whether they will find food to eat that day or whether they will have to resort to criminal acts to get their meals.

Nearly one hundred thousand youths in America live in cheap motel rooms. Many experience hunger and are exposed to drugs and criminal activities that are usually rampant in these underserved communities.

And they are constantly on the lookout for police officers who might arrest them for vagrancy. If they are arrested and under age eighteen, it is likely that authorities will send them to juvenile detention centers—essentially, jails for young people. Journalist Vivian Ho, who has written extensively on the plight of homeless young people, points out, "They have to keep moving before the cops show up or some business owner complains about them, shooing them off their sidewalks as if they were no better than the pigeons and vermin flocking among the garbage."[17]

> "They have to keep moving before the cops show up or some business owner complains about them, shooing them off their sidewalks as if they were no better than the pigeons and vermin flocking among the garbage."[17]
>
> —Vivian Ho, author *Those Who Wander*

Life on the streets for youths comes with an awareness that other people do not understand who they are or what their lives are like. It can mean that paying attention to what they wear on their feet might be the most important clothing choice of all. Some street youths favor steel-toed boots that can be an effective weapon if they need to defend themselves against assaults, thefts, abductions, or rape attempts.

Young people living on the streets make up the smallest percentage of homeless youth—the National Center on Family Homelessness estimates that about fifty-six thousand young people are unsheltered, meaning they have no homes in any definition of the word. Best-selling author Danielle Steel, who spent many years working with her own Yo! Angel! Foundation providing homeless people in San Francisco with warm clothing and food, says that she rarely encountered teenagers during her work among the homeless. This suggested to her that homeless young people are very good at hiding from police and even social workers who try to help them.

> Running into adolescents was rare for us. On one particular night we were in a back alley, and I can't remember if it was a tent or a pile of cardboard boxes we spotted, but out of

it emerged a couple of teenagers about sixteen or eighteen right out of a movie or CD cover on MTV. I had never seen such dazzling punk gear in my life: spikes and chains, leather and red plaid. The girl was wearing a pair of knee-high combat boots. [The boy] had a towering Mohawk that was glued into place. They had piercings and tattoos on every surface, but in their own crazy way, they were so beautiful to look at, and so extreme, that all of us smiled. We chatted with them for a while, gave them our stuff, and didn't intrude on them further. They wanted no additional help.[18]

Keeping Secrets

As Steel learned, many homeless youths do their best to keep other people from learning of their predicaments, hiding it from their teachers and friends. Trying to keep up appearances can be

Myths About the Homeless

Many people who enjoy secure homes harbor misconceptions about homeless young people. Such myths held by other people often make the day-to-day survival of homeless young people even more difficult because the myths add to their anxieties and often make them hesitant to reach out to others for help.

In 2020 the Mix, a British organization that provides charitable services for people under age twenty-five, conducted interviews with young people who had experienced homelessness during their lives. The young people were asked how they thought others perceived them. One former homeless young person, Kyle, said people considered him "lazy, troublesome, gang-affiliated, stupid, trampy, [and having] no life, no dreams or aspirations." Emily said the people she knew believed she was responsible for being homeless. She said people described her and other homeless young people as "problem children who are lazy. They are drug addicts and selfish." And Georgia said, "When I became homeless, I was told I was stupid, I was never going to get anywhere in life."

Quoted in Holly Turner, "Interview: How Do You Move on from Your Experience of Homelessness?," The Mix, July 29, 2020. www.themix.org.uk.

taxing. They might also want to protect their families from coming into contact with child protection services, which are government agencies with the authority to seek removal of children from abusive homes and dangerous living conditions.

When Desiree' LaMarr-Murphy was a public school student, she was often hungry but never shared that information with anyone. Her classmates ate lunch in the cafeteria as LaMarr-Murphy counted down the minutes until the period was over so she could stop thinking about food. Had she told someone, she would have been able to get free food, but she kept quiet. "I didn't want to make anyone in my family sad or feel bad, so I didn't talk about not eating lunch,"[19] LaMarr-Murphy says.

Han Johnson, now a high-achieving high school student, made a different decision in middle school. She elected to tell authorities about her situation. It did not go well. Desperate for help, she was only thirteen when she found the courage to tell a school social worker that she was afraid her mentally ill mother would attempt to kill her. She had, after all, been threatened by her mother with a knife. But instead of arranging the help she needed, the

Young people actually living on the streets make up the smallest percentage of homeless youth. It is estimated that fifty-six thousand young people are unsheltered.

social worker told Johnson that she did not believe anyone capable of earning top grades, as Johnson regularly did, could come from an abusive home.

With no help from the social worker, Johnson eventually took the only option she saw—running away and seeking a bed in a homeless shelter. "A lot of children have slipped through the cracks,"[20] she says. Johnson was able to graduate from high school and enrolled at Weber State University in Ogden, Utah. She lives in a dormitory, but between semesters, when the dormitories are closed, she must find a bed in a homeless shelter.

> "I didn't want to make anyone in my family sad or feel bad, so I didn't talk about not eating lunch."[19]
>
> —Desiree' LaMarr-Murphy, former food insecure child

Shelters May Be Scary

Shelters such as the facilities where Johnson often finds places to sleep are the only alternatives for many homeless young people. When there are no more friends or relatives to turn to or young people are living far from where they were raised, they may have no choice other than to seek beds in shelters.

Staying in a homeless shelter bears little resemblance to life in a private home. When Patrick was discharged from a mental health facility, the twenty-two-year-old was dropped off by staffers at a shelter in Seattle, Washington, designed for young adults with no other place to go. Life in the shelter came with rules. One of them was that everyone had to leave the shelter during the day. That meant Patrick had to find places to stay during the day until the nights-only shelter reopened its doors at 9:00 p.m. After rising from bed each morning at 7:00 a.m., Patrick filled his backpack with whatever he thought he would need for the day then left the shelter. He filled his free time with visits to parks, libraries, and other public spaces. After a week of living at the shelter, Patrick said, "I felt fine when I first got there and then it got progressively scarier for a while. . . . You aren't really living a life if you are living here."[21]

Patrick's sense of fear was a common emotion among young people navigating life without the help of caring parents. But even those who experience homelessness with their parents can be frightened as well. Christine sometimes lived in a motel with her sisters and her mother, a single parent and nurse who struggled to keep the family housed. The family had moved eighteen times, mostly staying in motels where criminal activity was a fact of life. In one motel room next to where her family was staying, a woman was murdered. Another time an attempt by police to make an arrest a few doors away led to an armed standoff. On another occasion Christine and her sisters were approached by thugs who wanted to turn them into prostitutes.

Anger and Shame

Along with fear, anger and shame are sometimes also experienced by homeless youths. They might wonder why other children and teens have it much easier, with lives untouched by food insecurity, mental illness, drug addiction, and domestic violence. Said one teen:

> Being homeless made me not only ashamed but angry— angry at my mother [who struggled with addiction], angry at myself, angry at the world—and I lashed out in every way I knew how. This monster that was homelessness ate away at me until I no longer cared about anyone or anything, until I became hardened to life and the things that happened to me. What I didn't realize then was that I should not have been angry or ashamed, and what I realize now is that I am not less than others just because I was homeless.[22]

Such feelings are understandable. What may be harder to understand, though, is that ultimately, young people in precarious home situations still have hope that their lives will improve. That was one of the findings of the Voices of Youth Count, a national study conducted by the University of Chicago in 2016 and 2017 in which more than twenty-six thousand adults, young adults, and teens were interviewed to identify how common youth

The Language of Homelessness

Words pack an emotional wallop. They can stigmatize and harm or uplift and inspire. Muhammad Tariq, a student journalist at the University of California, Davis, says it is important to pay attention to the words used to describe homelessness and addiction so that individuals to whom those words apply are not defined by them. He says, "Using the word 'person' first and their condition or situation last actively avoids the marginalization and dehumanization of people according to their condition or situation by enforcing their personhood before anything else."

An example of using person-first language as it applies to this context would be referring to someone as a person experiencing homelessness rather than labeling him or her as homeless. Tariq adds, "The word 'homeless' has become a blanket term that misrepresents a large, marginalized group of society. These are human beings, but they are being defined solely by their home 'ownership' status."

Muhammad Tariq, "It's Time to Start Using Person-First Language," *California Aggie* (Davis, CA), March 4, 2021. https://theaggie.org.

homelessness is in America. Said University of Chicago professor Shantá Robinson:

> The perception is that young people don't know what they want and we should just tell them. But they were very clear-eyed about what they needed—both what they needed to do themselves and the help they needed from outside. And there was very little hopelessness. They had wonderful, lofty aspirations for themselves. . . . The hope they had for themselves was profoundly encouraging.[23]

The study determined that whether young people live stable lives at home with their families or live in motels, homeless shelters, or on the streets, deep down they are all the same. All young people want to be loved and appreciated for who they are and to be understood for what they are going through. Young people who are homeless want nothing more.

CHAPTER 3

What Are the Consequences of Homelessness for Young People?

Erica, age seventeen, had been homeless for two years. After numerous clashes with her father and then her step-father, Erica finally ran away from her home in San Diego, California. At first she fled to Tijuana, Mexico, to live with her boyfriend's family, but American authorities tracked her down and took her back to California, where she was placed in a shelter for homeless youths.

Those two years were emotionally traumatic for Erica, but during the time she was on the run, she experienced another issue that faces most homeless young people: she did not attend school. This meant that when she returned to California and finally started classes again, she was two years behind other students her age.

Eventually, Erica was accepted into Monarch School, a school in San Diego devoted entirely to educating home-less young people. The programs at Monarch School are structured specifically for students like Erica who may have missed considerable class time during their months or years on the streets. Erica struggled to keep up with her studies. She was also facing the reality that when she turned eighteen she would be forced to leave the homeless shelter and, once again, be on her own. "I need support," she said in an interview just weeks before her eighteenth birthday. "It's the not knowing where I'm going to stay that keeps bringing me down. I don't know where I'm going to go."[24]

As Erica knew would happen, when she turned eighteen she was forced to leave the homeless shelter. She also stopped attending classes at Monarch School.

Educational Troubles

Missing school and falling behind on their studies is a consequence faced by many homeless young people. According to the San Diego County Office of Education, every time a young person moves to a new home, he or she falls four to six months behind others their own age in academic achievement. For a homeless young person, who over the course of a few years may move dozens of times—from motel room to motel room or homeless shelter to homeless shelter—this lack of stability could have a devastating effect on his or her ability to keep up with schoolwork. "Many of our students just don't know what it feels like to be successful,"[25] says Jessica Codallos, a counselor at Monarch School.

> "Many of our students just don't know what it feels like to be successful."[25]
>
> —Jessica Codallos, a counselor at Monarch School

A study by the National Center for Homeless Education compared proficiency in reading, mathematics, and science between homeless students and those who were considered economically disadvantaged but still enjoyed stable home lives. While both sets of scores left much room for improvement, homeless students fared far worse, averaging proficiency scores of 29 percent, 24 percent, and 26 percent in reading, math, and science, respectively, compared to 37 percent, 33 percent, and 35 percent for the economically disadvantaged.

When students fail to make progress in their classes or miss a lot of school because of instability in their home life, the risk of

not graduating from high school rises. According to statistics kept by Chapin Hall, an adult without a high school education is 346 percent more likely to be homeless than an adult who has graduated from high school or who has earned a general equivalency diploma (GED).

State governments that have looked at whether homeless youths are successful in earning a diploma typically find that about half of homeless young people graduate from high school or attain a GED. Among the states that have looked at the issue have been Washington, which found that 46 percent of homeless youths earn a diploma; Wyoming, where 53 percent of homeless young people graduated from high school; and Colorado, where the graduation rate among homeless youths was also 53 percent.

When homeless young people fail to earn at least a high school diploma, they face dim prospects for finding a job that will pay enough to enable them to find a place to live and afford groceries. Without a good job, they face the prospect of remaining homeless as they enter their adult years, creating a seemingly never-ending cycle of homelessness. If they go on to start their own family, their children may be homeless as well. And babies born to parents with housing instability often face health issues, such as malnutrition, that are not commonly faced by babies born into families that enjoy stable homes.

Juvenile Detention

Attending school is difficult for many homeless young people, but the consequences for skipping school may be harsh as well. In many states people under age eighteen who have not legally dropped out of school can be declared truant—meaning they can face arrest and find themselves in juvenile detention centers. Moreover, their parents may receive fines that they may not be able to pay, which could lead to their arrest as well. In Georgia, for example, students who have ten or more unexcused absences in one year may be flagged as children in need of state-mandated services, setting them on the path to foster care or detention. In New Jersey, students who refuse to attend school can be arrested and declared juvenile delinquents.

As a young runaway, Sheryl Recinos had a rude awakening when she ended up in a juvenile detention facility, just as her father had warned her that she would someday. After her arrest she was locked in a small cell in a concrete detention center. The cell featured a metal bed, thin mattress, thin sheets, no pillow, a metal sink, a metal toilet, and a window with bars on it.

> "I had been locked in a small cinderblock fortress and they took the keys with them. I didn't know if I should scream, or cry, or vomit."[26]
>
> —Sheryl Recinos, former homeless youth

The door to the cell allowed the guards to look in on her—robbing her of a measure of privacy. She recalls the gut-wrenching feeling of being trapped. "Every nerve fiber in my body was buzzing with a strange new sensation," she says. "I had been locked in a small cinderblock fortress and they took the keys with them. I didn't know if I should scream, or cry, or vomit. . . . I was a caged animal. I was trapped."[26]

Recinos's plight was not unusual. According to Casey Trupin, director of homelessness programs for the Seattle, Washington–based Raikes Foundation, some 44 percent of homeless youths have spent time in jail or juvenile detention centers. Once they have exposure to the justice system, it can be harder for youths to stay out of trouble or to feel good about themselves and their future, he says. And a criminal record will make it harder for them to find employment. Says Trupin, "This street-to-prison pipeline can derail a young person's life before it has even begun."[27]

Homeless and in College

Some homeless young people overcome the hurdles they face. They are able to avoid arrest, keep up with their studies, and go on to earn a high school diploma and even enter college. But for many homeless youths, the problems of homelessness even follow them onto their college campus. After they are accepted to college, they may find it difficult to afford textbooks—which can be expensive, even if students have been awarded financial aid or scholarships. Moreover, homeless college students may find dormitory life stable in that they have a place to sleep at night and dining halls to receive their meals, but during semester breaks and holidays, the campus dormitories and dining halls close. Very often, homeless college students have no place else to go until classes resume other than homeless shelters, the couches at friends' homes, or the streets.

As with their younger peers, homeless college students face extra challenges in getting their degree. While they have to study just as hard as their fellow students, they are more likely to have additional burdens. These may include lack of a stable internet connection and a quiet place to study as well as working to support themselves. Stressed and busy, they may have trouble sleeping and worry about how they are going to meet the requirements of their courses.

Sara Goldrick-Rab, a professor of higher-education policy at Temple University in Philadelphia, says the obligations carried by homeless students can be significant handicaps on their ability to excel in their classes. "It really undermines their ability to do well in school," she says. "Their grades suffer, their test scores appear to be lower, and overall, their chances of graduating are slimmer. They can barely escape their conditions of poverty long enough to complete their degrees."[28]

Alcohol and Drug Abuse

Finding ways to stay in school, keeping up with their studies, and managing to obtain a high school diploma or college degree are formidable tasks for homeless young people. But what makes those tasks even harder to achieve are the unwise solutions many homeless youths turn to in an effort to deal with their troubles.

Abusing alcohol or taking drugs are among the ways in which many young homeless people escape from their problems. Being homeless, on their own, and not knowing where they will sleep or when they will eat next leads many homeless youths to

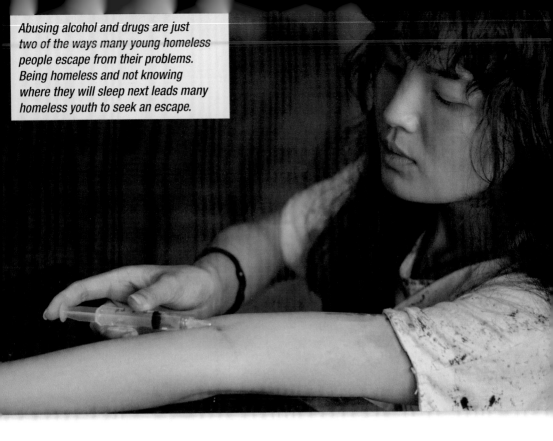

Abusing alcohol and drugs are just two of the ways many young homeless people escape from their problems. Being homeless and not knowing where they will sleep next leads many homeless youth to seek an escape.

seek an escape. Chapin Hall found that 29 percent of homeless youths have drug or alcohol problems. Chapin Hall's study found that some young people become homeless because they abuse drugs or alcohol. They leave their home as they search for a way to constantly stay high or drunk, or their families kick them out because of their addiction. Other young people develop an addiction once they find themselves without a home.

Samantha was placed in a group home in her native Canada as a teen when her mother could not care for her. She hated the home and sought to escape. She started using methamphetamine. This highly addictive drug hooks users because it makes them feel euphoric and less aware of what is going on around them. But its downsides are also potent: anxiety, insomnia, heartbeat irregularities, tooth decay, loss of appetite, and damage to the brain and major organs. Samantha took off from the group home for a week because of her addiction, as well as her desire to suppress her feelings about her situation. During that week on her own, she had no safe place to sleep. She says, "When I ran away I had nowhere to go. I would sleep on park benches sometimes, or not sleep at all. I would stay up all night on drugs. I remember there have been a couple times where I would end up sleeping in this parking garage on the bottom floor in this one corner."[29]

Victims of Human Trafficking

Young people like Samantha who are new to the street are particularly ripe for exploitation. They can be taken advantage of economically and bodily. Performing sexual acts for money can lead to arrest as well as exposure to sexually transmitted diseases. Young prostitutes can also become the victims of violent acts perpetrated by their customers or by their pimps, typically older males who employ them to provide sexual favors to customers. Research by

Medical Issues Homeless Teens Face

Dr. Seth Ammerman operates a mobile medical clinic in Northern California, offering free care, free medicine, and referrals to homeless teens. With the help of two nurses, he sees about four hundred patients a year. About 40 percent of them are homeless teens, some of whom have never seen a physician. One of them is Grace Kim, whom Ammerman first treated for substance abuse and malnutrition—problems associated with not having enough healthy food to eat. As part of Ammerman's treatment plan, Kim was referred to a psychiatrist who helped alleviate her depression and a nutritionist who found her the resources she needed to eat better.

Lack of healthy diet is a big problem for homeless teens. "If I didn't get that help, I would probably be in a very bad place. The whole mental health aspect of it was probably the most beneficial, probably the most powerful," Kim says. The help she received enabled her to enroll in a master's degree program in counseling psychology at Santa Clara University.

Quoted in Farida Jhabvala Romero, "Teen Health Van Delivers More than Medical Care to Homeless Youth," NPR, Feb. 17, 2016. www.npr.org.

the Harrisburg, Pennsylvania–based National Sexual Violence Resource Center has found that one in three teens begins resorting to prostitution within two days of starting their lives on the street.

While trading sex for money is a choice for some young people, others will be forced to perform sex acts against their will by human traffickers. Human traffickers are described by law enforcement officials as individuals who use physical force, fraud, or other forms of coercion to compel their victims to perform sex for money. A study by Loyola University in New Orleans, Louisiana, known as the Modern Slavery Research Project found that one out of five homeless youths in America and Canada have been trafficked. The group most likely to have been exposed to sex trafficking is homeless youths who identify as LGBTQ.

Human traffickers may also coerce homeless youths into selling drugs for them. More than 80 percent of forced labor among homeless young people involves drug sales, according to the Modern Slavery Research Project. As many young people learn, being arrested for selling drugs can carry severe consequences, including lengthy prison terms.

Victims of human trafficking can be left with physical and psychological problems, among them depression, anxiety, substance abuse, injuries caused by violence, and a deep mistrust of other people. Human traffickers isolate their victims by taking away their identification and cell phones, giving them no opportunities to seek help. These victims are forced to live under the authority of their traffickers, enduring threats of violence should they try to flee. To find new labor, human traffickers tend to lurk near drop-in shelters and parks where homeless youths gather.

Lacking a stable home increases the likelihood that young people will drop out of school and develop an addiction that brings them to the attention of the juvenile justice system, meaning they could wind up in a youth detention cell. Many young people become victims of sex traffickers. Lacking education, addicted to drugs or alcohol, or with a criminal arrest on their record, young people can be haunted by the consequences of homelessness well into adulthood.

CHAPTER 4

Safety Nets for Homeless Young People

Caryn and Nick were high school classmates in Shasta County, California. The two were dating when Caryn learned she was pregnant. At the time, Caryn was living with her grandparents—she had moved in with them because her parents were both drug abusers. "My parents were never in the picture," says Caryn. "I lived with my grandparents. My parents always chose drugs over their kids."[30]

But her grandparents greeted the news of Caryn's pregnancy with anger. They kicked her out of their house. Caryn was nineteen at the time. Nick was seventeen. They were unprepared to be on their own, moving often to a series of short-term accommodations: a trailer, an apartment, and brief stays with Nick's mother and father.

Weary of enduring the physical burdens of being pregnant and moving frequently, Caryn told a teacher of her plight and found the help she needed. The connection was made through the school's liaison for homeless students, a staff member who was able to assist the couple in finding financial aid, free food programs, and temporary housing. Such help made it possible for Caryn and Nick to earn their high school diplomas and receive instruction on how to be good parents to their child and maintain their own household.

School liaisons are social workers whose job is to connect homeless students with desperately needed services for food, shelter, and clothing, among other needs. But they can only assist students if they are willing to accept help and admit that they—and possibly their parents—are having problems. Stacy Watson, a transitional youth case manager at Hill Country Health and Wellness Center in Redding, California, which provides a variety of medical and behavioral health counseling services to teens, often interacts with young homeless people. She says, "Now people are aware of the program and now some of the kids come up to me on their own and talk to me and say, 'Hey, are you the homeless helping lady?'"[31]

Student Advocacy Center

For homeless youths to find services that are available to them, they must come in contact with caring adults who know which services are available and how they can be acquired. DaQuann Harrison's experience as a homeless youth in Detroit, Michigan, began when he was a young child. Harrison's mother was in an abusive relationship with a boyfriend at the time. Soon, she and Harrison fled her boyfriend's home and for the next several years spent their nights in cars, shopping malls, and motels. Harrison turned to crime early, shoplifting food in grocery stores in order to eat. Finally, Harrison was arrested after he carried an air gun and knife to school to defend himself against bullies.

He spent three days in juvenile detention but was released by a judge who could tell that Harrison needed guidance in his life. A parole officer was assigned to his case. A parole officer is employed by the courts and assigned to people who have been incarcerated and served their time but face supervision as a condition of their release.

Harrison's parole officer told him about a program he could access through the Student Advocacy Center of Michigan in Detroit. The advocacy center's purpose is to keep students in school so they can complete their education. One way the center does that is by providing mentors. A mentor is a person who agrees to counsel another person. Very often the mentors have had similar life experiences and can help guide young people through the difficult life decisions they have to make.

Harrison was initially skeptical about the program but was willing to give it a try. "I was suspicious at first because I'm an independent person," he says. "But I'm glad I took that step because my mentor, Anell Eccleston, is truly the best thing that happened to me in a very, very long time. I believe we made an unbreakable bond, and that's what I have been wanting all my life."[32]

Harrison's mentor spent a lot of time with him. They engaged in regular weekly meetings—sometimes meeting several times a week—to address Harrison's needs. Harrison knew he could depend on Eccleston to help him find food, clothing, and transportation; finish high school; and even complete college applications. Eccleston was not the only person in Harrison's corner. He soon

School liaisons are social workers whose job is to connect homeless students with desperately needed services for food, shelter, clothing, and other requirements.

American Idol Teen Singer Was Homeless

In the 2021 season of the reality TV show *American Idol*, nineteen-year-old Ronda Felton moved music legend Lionel Ritchie, one of the show's judges, to tears as she sang a song from the movie and play *Dreamgirls.* For Felton, of Milwaukee, Wisconsin, this was a dream moment. Music had been her salvation during the five years she had lived with her mother in homeless shelters, or their car, or slept on friends' couches.

By the time she was fifteen, Felton had attended twelve different schools. During that period her mother had worked at several jobs, hoping to save enough money so that they could get a place of their own. Felton said: "My mom used to sing and she used to make us sing certain songs and make sure our pitches were correct. (Life) was very hectic, so music . . . was something that I didn't have to deal with necessarily. It wasn't something that was an added stress. Music was something where I could go somewhere and didn't have to be myself. I could be someone else."

Before her appearance on *Idol*, she participated in musical theater. "I wasn't aspiring to be a singer or aspiring to be an actor," Felton said. "It's just that I wanted a way out."

Quoted in Piet Levy, "From Homelessness to 'American Idol,' Milwaukee Native Ronda Felton Looks Toward Her Future," *Milwaukee Journal Sentinel*, April 6, 2021. www.jsonline.com.

found that many people were invested in his success. He says, "When I finally returned to high school, I had so many people nagging me. Anell, someone from the sheriff's office, staff at other organizations who helped me, and a bunch of staff from a [school] district where I wasn't even a student. They drove me nuts. But I went to school."[33]

Help from the Community

As Harrison's experience illustrates, an important ingredient in helping someone find his or her way out of homelessness is for the homeless person to form relationships with people who are not homeless and are willing to help. "It takes a village," says Harrison. "It takes love, hope, consistent persistence, and support for each student. We need relationships that last, and we need a lot of them. We, as a society, can't give up on homeless teens like me."[34]

Even young children can be part of that village, as seven-year-old Olivia Dru Tyler of Arlington Heights in suburban Chicago has proved. Since at age five, Olivia has shown unusual empathy for homeless people, sometimes giving them money. But she told her parents that she wanted to do more. Olivia's parents decided to take action on their daughter's passion to help the homeless during the COVID-19 pandemic. Shortly after the pandemic struck, government officials in Illinois ordered all residents to wear fabric face masks outside their homes to reduce the possibility that they would spread the viral infection to others. When Olivia heard of the restriction, she knew the disease could severely impact homeless people because they would not have the money to buy face masks. "How will homeless people get covered?" Olivia asked her mother, Linda Tyler. After Olivia posed that question, Linda said to herself, "OK, I need to pay attention to this."[35]

> "We, as a society, can't give up on homeless teens like me."[34]
>
> —DaQuann Harrison, Detroit parolee

Linda and Olivia's father, Andrew, got to work. They created the nonprofit group OliviaDruCares, then recruited other qualified adults to sit on a board of directors to run it. Her parents are bringing the right life skills to the project. Andrew owns a digital media and film company—and he spent some years as a homeless teen and therefore has firsthand knowledge of the challenges facing homeless young people. Linda is a professional fundraiser for medical institutions, an occupation that has been a huge asset for a nonprofit organization trying to raise money for a good cause. During 2020 OliviaDruCares started selling fabric face masks to consumers for five dollars each, then donating a face mask for each sale to homeless people.

Help for Runaways

Community-based organizations have done more than provide fabric face masks for homeless people. One group, the

Chicago-based National Runaway Safeline, provides a toll-free hotline for young people to call if they are thinking of leaving home or have already done so. It is available for young people in the Chicago area and across the country as well. Young people can phone, text, live chat, or email the National Runaway Safeline.

The hotline aims to keep young people safe. Its services are funded through private donations as well as the Family and Youth Services Bureau in the Administration for Children, Youth and Families, part of the US Department of Health and Human Services. The National Runaway Safeline connects young people to a variety of services, including mental health counseling, child abuse services, help with housing, and issues faced by LGBTQ youths and young victims of human trafficking. In 2019, 55 percent of the youths the hotline assisted had been on the street a week or less, while 28 percent had been on their own for a month or more.

Moreover, in partnership with Greyhound Lines, the national bus company, in 2020 the National Runaway Safeline provided

In 2020, the organization National Runaway Safeline, in partnership with bus company Greyhound (pictured), provided nearly three hundred youths with free bus tickets to return home during the COVID-19 pandemic.

nearly three hundred youths free bus tickets to return home during the COVID-19 pandemic. Anyone age twelve to twenty-one who was homeless, a runaway, or a victim of human trafficking could receive bus tickets to their home cities.

And there are many other community-based organizations as well. A homeless youth named Liam found help at Safe Place in Louisville, Kentucky, when he was kicked out of his home following a fight with a family member. Safe Place is a community-based organization composed of local places that agree to provide shelters for homeless young people. Such shelters are often provided by libraries, fire stations, private businesses, and YMCAs. In fact, Safe Place stickers are pasted onto their front doors—telling homeless young people they have found a safe place to stay. As a result of visiting a Safe Place, Liam spent a week in a youth shelter, which gave his family time to recover from the incident that led to Liam's banishment. The youth shelter staff assisted the family in coming up with a reunification plan, enabling Liam to return home. Had Liam not found refuge through Safe Place, it is likely he would have continued wandering the streets.

Transitional Living Programs

Ultimately, Liam did return home, but in many cases homeless young people do not have that option. Their families are dysfunctional and often violent, and it is likely they would not be safe if they did return home. However, because they lack the skills to live on their own—to get their high school diploma or GED, find vocational training, handle money, run a household, buy and cook food, purchase clothing, find health care, handle relationships, or receive psychological counseling—they need a bridge between childhood and the independence of adulthood. Transitional living programs can provide that bridge for young people ages sixteen to twenty-two. These young people often need to master skills to help them become self-supporting adults. Through its Family and Youth Services Bureau, the federal government provides funding for such assistance through group homes, including those for expectant mothers or young mothers, host-family homes, and apartments. These services can be used by young people for as long as eighteen months.

Jason Bennan entered a transitional living program in Staten Island, New York, when he was twenty years old. At that point, Bennan was too old to continue in the foster care system and had served time in jail for stealing a truck. While in jail, he found that it was a violent place where gang membership was a means of survival. When he was stabbed in a fight, Bennan knew he had to change his life. He said, "I thought to myself, 'I don't want to be in jail, and I have to do things the right way—even though it's hard.'"[36]

Bennan applied to a transitional housing program and was placed in a multifamily group home, where he had to abide by

Keeping Families in Their Homes Saves Money

What would happen if families received the financial help they needed before they lost their homes due to financial instability? In Washington State, a three-year pilot program run by a coalition of nearly twenty organizations called Priority Spokane was set up in 2016 to test that question. The group focused on helping families in three elementary schools and one middle school. In each of those schools, they installed a community health care worker to identify at-risk families and to offer them individualized help with their unique life situations. In one case the help needed was as simple as seventy-two dollars to repair the family car so it could be driven to work and income could keep coming in.

So far, the program has helped nearly three hundred students remain in their homes. As of 2019, 95 percent of those families were still housed. The total expenditure per family was less than $10,000. The program was so successful that it was extended another two years. Executive director Ryan Oelrich says the program has proved that it costs much less to keep families together and in their own homes than to find them new places to live after they become homeless. He says, "We absolutely know that we save money housing folks. There's no doubt."

Quoted in Chris Julin, "Students on the Move: The Growing Crisis of Homeless Kids," APM Reports, August 14, 2019. www.apmreports.org.

some strict rules. Security cameras kept watch on his every move as well as those of his fellow residents. When he needed help, a social worker was available. He had to get used to living with multiple roommates as well. Still, the arrangement worked for him. Now when he fills out a job application, Bennan can say that he is a high school graduate, and with that credential, he was able to get a job in a grocery store, providing him with a steady income.

> "I thought to myself, 'I don't want to be in jail, and I have to do things the right way— even though it's hard.'"[36]
>
> —Jason Bennan, former transitional living resident

His social worker, Jason Maniscalco, worked closely with Bennan. "With young adults, there's still an opportunity to reach them," says Maniscalco. Although they might not always follow the suggestions, there is value in connecting with these young people. "Whether they listen to you or not, for me, that's where the reward is."[37]

As Bennan's social worker pointed out, homeless teens may have more options than they realize. Many of those options are offered by community-based groups that want to get homeless young people off the streets and help them restart their lives.

CHAPTER 5

Bouncing Back from Homelessness

Sharday Hamilton had her first baby at age eighteen, trying to do her best to raise her daughter while the two lived in an abandoned house in Chicago. By the time the baby was taken away from her by a social services agency, Hamilton was expecting her second child. After her baby boy was born, Hamilton and the child were able to find space at a homeless shelter. Five years later, Hamilton transitioned from needing the services of a shelter to working as a peer-outreach professional helping other people navigate through the homelessness maze and obtain much-needed services.

Part of her job is to seek out homeless people on Chicago streets and offer them help. She often walks the streets with other social workers at night. "I talk to a lot of women," she says. "When I go looking, I go looking for mothers, young people with kids. They feel more comfortable talking to me. I'm able to share my story. . . . A lot of people are afraid of judgment. It's relatable to me when a youth says they don't want services, because that's how I was. But look at me now, now I have housing."[38]

There are many success stories among formerly homeless young people. They have grown into adults and want to be part of the solution to homelessness. Carissa Phelps is another example. The former sex trafficking victim, drug addict, and prison inmate went on to earn a law degree and created Runaway Girl Inc., an organization that provides opportunities for career education and leadership to runaways, former runaways, and other homeless young people. She also lobbies for legislative reforms that benefit homeless youths. "That child in the mirror—she survived," says Phelps. "And now that I can see her looking back at me, I am able to love her for the first time. She is the child in me who seeks happiness and helps me keep balance in a sometimes crazy and backward world."[39]

> "When I go looking, I go looking for mothers, young people with kids. They feel more comfortable talking to me. I'm able to share my story."[38]
>
> —Sharday Hamilton, former homeless teen mother

Being a Parent

Other formerly homeless young people have gone on to contribute to society in other ways. Desperate to escape a father she hated, Sheryl Recinos stole money from him and ran away multiple times beginning at age thirteen. She spent time on the streets and in juvenile detention, group homes, and foster care. Today Recinos is a family physician who is especially adept at handling the care of children enduring similar ordeals.

For Recinos, the way out of homelessness began when she gave birth as a teenager. Knowing that she would be responsible for another human being was the impetus she needed to take better care of herself and plan for a future. Recinos proudly owns all the hardships she went through because she believes she would not be the person she is today had she not gone through them. She says:

It's been a whirlwind looking back at where it all began, but it's also been amazing to realize that because of what I went through, I became a better mother and human than I could've ever imagined. My kids are compassionate, decent people who care about others. As I've seen them

45

grow up, their normal experiences have reinforced for me why I had to survive such difficult times. I am grateful for the journey, and I will continue paying it forward.[40]

Prison Recovery

Recinos ultimately succeeded because she set goals for herself and was determined to achieve them. Similarly, a former New York City prison inmate named Albert was able to lift himself out of a life of crime because he finally set goals for himself and worked toward meeting those goals.

After his first arrest Albert quit school, left home, and spent three years on the streets, supporting himself by committing crimes. He was frequently arrested and locked up—so much so that he began to feel at home in jail. It was, he decided, a much easier life than fending for himself on the streets.

But the revolving door between prison and freedom and back again finally came to an end. Albert eventually made contact with Ready, Willing & Able, a New York City organization that helps

There are many success stories among formerly homeless young people. Some have gone on to become doctors, making them especially adept at handling the care of youths who are facing similar ordeals.

A Tale of Two Sisters

Abaynee Carr did not grow up with her sister but reconnected with her as an adult. When the two met, Carr immediately realized how lucky she was to have been adopted by a loving family. Her sister had not been so lucky. She could not endure foster care and ran away. On her own, she became a victim of human traffickers.

Now a principal at Compton Bridge Academy, a Los Angeles–based charter school, Carr sees her sister in the faces of the homeless students she comes into contact with. Mindful that the system failed her sibling, Carr created Haven's House, a nonprofit organization that connects homeless young people to sources for clothes, therapy, and shelter. It is her attempt to assist the sixty-six thousand homeless students residing in her county who require services. She says:

> Sometimes it's not that their parents aren't there or can't be there, sometimes they just don't have the tools also, or they don't know where to get the resources to help make their child successful or them get through school. . . . We're here to help those families, those students, to make sure that, just like my sister, there is somebody who's there to help them if the system has failed them.

Quoted in Loureen Ayyoub, "Compton Principal Creates Nonprofit to Help Homeless Youth," Spectrum News 1, March 4, 2021. https://spectrumnews1.com.

former inmates start new lives. Ready, Willing & Able helped Albert achieve his goal of becoming a long-distance truck driver, ferrying goods across the country. Says Albert, "When I look back now, I see that I spent so much time just doing the same things. Going back to those same streets, committing the same crimes, just running in circles and going nowhere. . . . I'm ready to get in that truck and start driving."[41]

Unlikely Allies

For Albert, learning how to be a long-distance truck driver provided a path out of homelessness. Leslie Adindu found a much different path out of homelessness: the football field.

Born in Nigeria and brought to Fort Worth, Texas, as a teen by his father, Adindu was facing difficult times for an eighteen-year-old. Not only did he have to adjust to life in America, but he suffered another blow when his father abandoned him for work in another state. Adindu ended up in a homeless shelter at night while attending high school by day. But his athletic physique caught the attention of the school's football coaches, who talked the 6-foot, 4-inch (193 cm) tall, 190-pound (86 kg) teen into joining the team even though Adindu had never played the sport.

He worked hard to be a productive member of the junior varsity team. But then age nearly derailed him. When Adindu turned nineteen, he was no longer eligible to play high school football. But his coaches offered him a bargain. As long as he continued to come to school and football practice, they promised to use their influence to get college coaches to consider him for a scholarship. Adindu carried out his end of the bargain and so did his coaches. Impressed by what they saw in him, coaches at Southwest Baptist University in Bolivar, Missouri, offered him a football scholarship. Adindu enrolled in the college and joined the team as a defensive tackle. "Don't give up," he advises other homeless youths. "Most people would have given up [in my situation]. Just don't give up. Do the best you can."[42]

> "Don't give up. Most people would have given up [in my situation]. Just don't give up. Do the best you can."[42]
>
> —Leslie Adindu, former homeless teen

Professional Football

While there is no questioning Adindu's achievement in going from being homeless to playing college football, a similar and perhaps even more impressive achievement belongs to Josh Jacobs, who went from homeless teen to a first-round pick in the National Football League by the Oakland Raiders. Raised by his father in Tulsa, Oklahoma, during the time when he was in the fourth through eighth grades, Jacobs as well as his sister and three brothers slept in motels or in his father's car until his father was able to find

Josh Jacobs (pictured) went from homeless teen to a first-round draft pick playing for the Oakland Raiders. Jacobs, as well as his three brothers and sister, were homeless for many years during their childhood.

steady work. Despite not having enough to eat, clean clothes, or a place to shower other than the school locker room throughout his homeless years, Jacobs knew his father loved him. His family life was surprisingly lighthearted and happy, and Jacobs paid attention to the lessons his father taught him—especially the lessons about perseverance.

Jacobs plays running back—a position that requires him to carry the football, catch passes from the quarterback, and block members of the opposing team. As a player, Jacobs is known for his blazing running style. He says:

People say I run angry. I don't know. I guess I do. But I honestly don't think it's about how I run. It's about why I do it, and who I do it for. I run for my pops, the man who sacrificed so much and worked so hard to provide for me and educate me. I run for my three-year-old son, Braxton, so he can have a father he's proud of, like I'm proud of mine. I run for my sister and my three brothers. I run for my team-mates and my coaches. I run for everybody who has ever supported me, anyone who's ever doubted me, and for anyone out there living on white rice and ramen noodles. I run for anyone who's in a tough situation and feels like it's never going to end—that there's no light at the end of the tunnel. I run to show them that there is. Then, when I'm to-tally spent—when I'm on my last leg and I have absolutely nothing left to give . . . I dig even deeper. And I run for me.[43]

Excelling in Academics

Philadelphia teenager Richard Jenkins was also able to call on his own talents to help him out of a homeless life. Unlike Jacobs and Adindu, his talent was not on the football field. Rather, Jenkins's talent was excellence in academics. Growing up, he spent time in a homeless shelter and as he got older was admitted to Girard College, a boarding school for disadvantaged youths.

In elementary school he experienced a moment of clarity when a classmate asked him if he resided at a shelter. Jenkins lied and said he did not. "I was so embarrassed to say I lived in a shelter. But that's when I real-ized I got to buckle in because I can't have my potential kids going through what I am going through now,"[44] he says.

> "I was so embarrassed to say I lived in a shelter. But that's when I realized I got to buckle in because I can't have my potential kids going through what I am going through now."[44]
>
> —Richard Jenkins, Harvard student

Jenkins's studious nature was so well known that some classmates scornfully addressed him as "Harvard," somehow guessing his secret ambition of getting into the elite Ivy League school in Cambridge, Massachusetts. But that is what hap-pened. While enrolled at Girard, Jenkins received a letter from the prestigious university saying he had been admitted to the school. Moreover, Harvard awarded Jenkins a full-tuition scholarship, en-abling him to pursue a degree in computer science.

Training Dogs and People

At an animal shelter in Detroit, Michigan, a small pit bull and a nineteen-year-old homeless youth named Robyn Wesley were involved in a mutually beneficial arrangement involving work and play. The latter was serious business for both of them.

The pit bull, named Nugget, was not fully informed about the plan and did not realize he was learning skills that he would need to be adopted. Nugget faced stiff competition from the other three hundred dogs awaiting adoption. If he could learn how to sit, come when called, and walk on a leash, he might be more adoptable.

Wesley was living in a youth shelter and participating in the Teacher's Pet Program with full knowledge that the skills she was picking up could be used to find work as a dog trainer. She was one of just seven eighteen- to twenty-four-year-olds in the ten-year-old program. "When I first came in," Wesley says, "tears dropped from my eyes. I had an instant connection with the dogs." After completing the program, Wesley would be able to earn money helping other people learn ways to control their pets' behaviors.

Quoted in Meira Gebel, "I Didn't Know a Dog Could Be Your Best Friend," *Holland (MI) Sentinel*, January 5, 2019, p. 7.

Eliminating Youth Homelessness

As the tales of Jenkins, Jacobs, and Adindu illustrate, it is not difficult to find stories of formerly homeless teens who not only survived but ended up thriving. But it is also easy to uncover stories of teens whose lives were shortened or forever traumatized by their circumstances. While each story is unique and each set of circumstances leading to homelessness is at least slightly different, together they represent a complex societal problem that must be solved. The lack of affordable housing and affordable postsecondary education opportunities, the prevalence of low-paying jobs that do not sustain a family's needs, and the challenges of receiving appropriate mental health care all play a part in homelessness in general.

Larkin Street Youth Services, a San Francisco, California–based provider of services for young people experiencing homelessness, is upbeat in its belief that youth homelessness can be

Teen homelessness is a complex societal problem that must be solved. Many factors, including the lack of affordable housing and affordable postsecondary education, contribute to homelessness.

made rare and brief. In a 2020 report, the organization offered some steps for achieving that goal, beginning with collecting better data on homeless youth and using that data to drive programming and policy. The report also suggested that young people who know the issue firsthand be given a greater voice in advocating for policy changes, particularly LGBTQ and minority youths who make up a disproportionate share of the youth homeless population.

Another optimist is Ryan J. Dowd, executive director of the Hesed homeless shelter near Chicago. He says:

> Homelessness is not inevitable. It did not always exist. The current phenomenon of homelessness, as we understand it today, did not exist until about 40 years ago. . . . Very few shelters existed before 1980; now they are everywhere.

Homelessness is a very modern invention, and is the con-fluence of bad policies and shifting societal attitudes about family responsibility. If we can create homelessness in a matter of decades, is it really absurd to think that we can't end it in the same amount of time?[45]

Homelessness is a problem that can very well be solved. It would take the resources of governmental agencies, certainly, as well as the efforts of community-based organizations. But it will also take a change in attitude by many people who are homeless. They need to stop thinking of their situations as hopeless and to adopt the attitudes of people like Sharday Hamilton, Carissa Phelps, Leslie Adindu, and Richard Jenkins—that they very much do have the skills and desire to succeed in society.

SOURCE NOTES

Introduction: Hiding in Plain Sight

1. Quoted in Alfred Lubrano, "Homeless Teens in Philly Tap Rough Memories to Help Others Understand Their Lives," *Philadelphia (PA) Inquirer*, July 19, 2019. www.inquirer.com.
2. Quoted in Shawn Radcliffe, "Meet the New Face of Homelessness: Children and Teens," Healthline, October 20, 2018. www.healthline.com.
3. Quoted in Mihir Zaveri, "Is Youth Homelessness Going Up or Down? It Depends on Whom You Ask," *New York Times*, March 24, 2020. www.nytimes.com.
4. Quoted in Zaveri, "Is Youth Homelessness Going Up or Down?"
5. Quoted in Lubrano, "Homeless Teens in Philly Tap Rough Memories to Help Others Understand Their Lives."

Chapter 1: Why Do Some Young People Lack Homes?

6. Quoted in Voices of Youth Count, "Missed Opportunities: Youth Homelessness in America," 2017. https://voicesof youthcount.org.
7. Quoted in Voices of Youth Count, "Missed Opportunities."
8. Nick Seip, "New Report Underlines Role of Family in Preventing Youth Homelessness," True Colors United, September 14, 2016. https://truecolorsunited.org.
9. Quoted in Matt Turner, "Black, Queer, Homeless Youth. West Village Kids," *Huck*, September 23, 2020. www.huckmag.com.
10. Quoted in Sarah Carter Narendorf and Charles Batiste, "To Solve Youth Homelessness We Must Make Race Part of the Equation," *Youth Today*, July 17, 2019. https://youthtoday.org.
11. Quoted in Susanne Babbel, "The Foster Care System and Its Victims: Part 2," *Somatic Psychology* (blog), *Psychology Today*, January 3, 2012. www.psychologytoday.com.
12. Quoted in Your Teen, "Teenage Homelessness Stories: Shame, Fear and Uncertainty," 2019. https://yourteenmag.com.

13. Ryan J. Dowd, *The Librarian's Guide to Homelessness: An Empathy-Driven Approach to Solving Problems, Preventing Conflict, and Serving Everyone*. Chicago, IL: American Library Association, 2018, p. 196.

Chapter 2: What Is It like to Be a Homeless Teen?

14. Quoted in Joe Mozingo, "No Room at the Inn for Innocence," *Los Angeles Times*, July 22, 2015. https://graphics.latimes.com.
15. Quoted in Mozingo, "No Room at the Inn for Innocence."
16. Quoted in Jeff Karabanow et al., *Homeless Youth and the Search for Stability*. Waterloo, ON: Wilfrid Laurier University Press, 2018, p. 36.
17. Vivian Ho, *Those Who Wander: America's Lost Street Kids*. New York: Little A, 2019, p. 175.
18. Danielle Steel, *A Gift of Hope: Helping the Homeless*. New York: Delacorte Press, 2012, p. 89.
19. Quoted in Alfred Lubrano, "Food Pantry: Teacher Overcame Hard Times. Now She Helps Others from Her Home," *Philadelphia (PA) Inquirer*, February 11, 2021, p. B1.
20. Quoted in Stell Simonton, "Formerly Homeless Youth Urge Congress to Act During Pandemic," *Youth Today*, July 23, 2020. https://youthtoday.org.
21. Quoted in Allegra Abramo, "After Leaving Addiction Treatment, Young Adults Often Face Homelessness," Crosscut, July 22, 2020. https://crosscut.com.
22. Quoted in Your Teen, "Teenage Homelessness Stories."
23. Quoted in Mark Sheehy, "Uncovering the Story of Youth Homelessness," *SSA Magazine*, Spring 2018. https://crownschool.uchicago.edu.

Chapter 3: What Are the Consequences of Homelessness for Young People?

24. Quoted in Eilene Zimmerman, "A High School for the Homeless," *The Atlantic*, June 16, 2015. www.theatlantic.com.
25. Quoted in Zimmerman, "A High School for the Homeless."
26. Sheryl Recinos, *Hindsight: Coming of Age on the Streets of Hollywood*. Los Angeles, CA: Recinos, 2018, p. 61.
27. Casey Trupin, "We Must Work to End America's Youth Homelessness Problem," *The Hill* (Washington, DC), January 12, 2018. https://thehill.com.
28. Quoted in Vanessa Romo, "Hunger and Homelessness Are Widespread Among College Students, Study Finds," NPR, April 3, 2018. www.npr.org.

29. Quoted in Eva's Initiatives for Homeless Youth, "Samantha's Story," November 25, 2020. www.evas.ca.

Chapter 4: Safety Nets for Homeless Young People

30. Quoted in Nada Atieh, "Homeless Youths Face Struggles in Shasta County. Here's One Couple's Story," *Redding (CA) Record Searchlight*, January 4, 2021. www.redding.com.
31. Quoted in Atieh, "Homeless Youths Face Struggles in Shasta County."
32. DaQuann Harrison, "Homeless Teens: How This One Became a College Student," Your Teen, 2019. https://yourteenmag.com.
33. Harrison, "Homeless Teens."
34. Harrison, "Homeless Teens."
35. Quoted in Marie Wilson, "Her Help for Homeless Masks Larger Charitable Goal," *Arlington Heights (IL) Daily Herald*, June 4, 2020, p. 1.
36. Quoted in Kyle Lawson, "From Jailhouse Stabbing to a GED: Ex-Foster Kid Fights to Put Life Back on Track," *Staten Island (NY) Advance*, January 29, 2017. www.silive.com.
37. Quoted in Lawson, "From Jailhouse Stabbing to a GED."

Chapter 5: Bouncing Back from Homelessness

38. Sharday Hamilton, "The Night Ministry," Chicago Foundation for Women, 2018. https://daring.cfw.org.
39. Carissa Phelps, *Runaway Girl: Escaping Life on the Streets, One Helping Hand at a Time*. New York: Viking, 2012, p. 287.
40. Recinos, *Hindsight*, p. 376.
41. Quoted in Ready, Willing & Able, "I'm Still Working on the Man I Want to Be, but Now I Know Exactly How to Achieve My Dreams," 2021. www.doe.org/albert.
42. Quoted in Meghan Overdeep, "Texas Teen Overcomes Homelessness to Receive Football Scholarship," *Southern Living*, February 9, 2021. http://southernliving.com.
43. Josh Jacobs, "People Say I Run Angry," Players' Tribune, April 25, 2019. www.theplayerstribune.com.
44. Quoted in AP News, "Once Homeless Philadelphia Teen Gets Full Ride to Harvard," May 23, 2018. https://apnews.com.
45. Dowd, *The Librarian's Guide to Homelessness*, p. 238.

ORGANIZATIONS AND WEBSITES

Chapin Hall at the University of Chicago

www.chapinhall.org

Chapin Hall at the University of Chicago works with government, nonprofits, philanthropists, and others to research challenges experienced by children and families. Its website offers reports on homelessness and foster care youth, ways the pandemic is affecting families, and more.

Covenant House

www.covenanthouse.org

The nonprofit Covenant House offers housing and support services to seventy-four thousand young people each year. Its website offers information on the factors that lead to youth homelessness and how Covenant House is addressing them and shares stories of teens who have benefited from the agency's services.

DoSomething

www.dosomething.org

DoSomething describes itself as a global movement of young people making positive change. Homelessness and poverty are two of the many social ills the organization deals with. Students can find information on understanding youth homelessness, a sheet containing eleven facts about homeless teens, and multiple ways students can get involved with helping out local homeless shelters.

National Alliance to End Homelessness

https://endhomelessness.org

The National Alliance to End Homelessness is a nonpartisan, nonprofit organization working to prevent and end homelessness in the United States. Its website offers information on the causes of homelessness, solutions for addressing it, data and graphics on the issues surrounding it, and the *State of Homelessness 2020* report.

National Homelessness Law Center

https://nlchp.org

Based in Washington, DC, the National Homelessness Law Center strives to end and prevent homelessness. In 2018 the center won its case in front of the US Court of Appeals for the Ninth Circuit, in which it argued that criminalizing the act of sleeping outside on public property was cruel and unusual punishment if there were no viable alternatives. The website offers ideas on how students can do their part.

National Runaway Safeline

www.1800runaway.org

National Runaway Safeline is a fifty-year-old organization that connects young people to a variety of services, including mental health counseling, child abuse services, help with housing, and issues faced by LGBTQ youths and young victims of human trafficking. It offers a twenty-four-hour hotline accessible at 1-800-RUNAWAY to teens in crisis and also accepts texts and live chat requests.

FOR FURTHER RESEARCH

Books

Cherese Cartlidge, *Homeless Youth*. San Diego, CA: Reference-Point, 2017.

Randy Christensen, *Ask Me Why I Hurt: The Kids Nobody Wants and the Doctor Who Heals Them*. New York: Broadway, 2011.

Brian J. Dowd, *The Librarian's Guide to Homelessness: An Empathy-Driven Approach to Solving Problems, Preventing Conflict, and Serving Everyone*. Chicago, IL: American Library Association, 2018.

Vivian Ho, *Those Who Wander: America's Lost Street Kids*. New York: Little A, 2019.

Jeff Karabanow et al., *Homeless Youth and the Search for Stability*. Waterloo, ON: Wilfrid Laurier University Press, 2018.

C. Nicole Mason, *Born Bright: A Young Girl's Journey from Nothing to Something in America*. New York: St. Martin's, 2016.

Sheryl Recinos, *Hindsight: Coming of Age on the Streets of Hollywood*. Los Angeles, CA: Recinos, 2018.

Lauren Sandler, *This Is All I Got: A New Mother's Search for Home*. New York: Random House, 2020.

Jim Wahlberg, *The Big Hustle: A Boston Street Kid's Story of Addiction and Redemption*. Huntington, IN: Our Sunday Visitor, 2020.

Internet Sources

Nada Atieh, "Homeless Youths Face Struggles in Shasta County. Here's One Couple's Story," *Redding (CA) Record Searchlight*, January 4, 2021. www.redding.com.

Loureen Ayyoub, "Compton Principal Creates Nonprofit to Help Homeless Youth," Spectrum News 1, March 4, 2021. https://spectrumnews1.com.

Mary Kate Bacalao, "For Homeless Youth, Surviving Is a Crime," Juvenile Justice Information Exchange, August 23, 2019. https://jjie.org.

E.A. Gjelten, "Truancy Laws: The Legal Consequences of Skipping School," Lawyers.com, February 5, 2019. www.lawyers.com.

Suzette Hackney, "Driven to Tell the Stories of America's Forgotten Homeless," *USA Today*, September 15, 2020. www.usatoday.com.

Vanessa Romo, "Hunger and Homelessness Are Widespread Among College Students, Study Finds," NPR, April 3, 2018. www.npr.org.

Kevin Ryan, "Homeless Kids Count. Count Them Correctly," CNBC, February 13, 2015. www.cnbc.com.

Stell Simonton, "Formerly Homeless Youth Urge Congress to Act During Pandemic," *Youth Today*, July 23, 2020. https://youthtoday.org.

Lauren Young, "Young Homeless People Are Struggling to Stay Safe During the Pandemic," *Teen Vogue*, June 4, 2020. www.teenvogue.com.

INDEX

PICTURE CREDITS